Paul's Gospel of Love

Gary W

Senior Fellow in Nev ollege

GROVE BOOKS LIMITED
RIDLEY HALL RD CAMBRIDGE CB3 9HU

Contents

Acknowledgments

My thanks to Ian Paul and Michael B Thompson for the encouragement to write this booklet and to colleagues who took the time to provide valuable feedback.

Note

Most Bible references are from the New Revised Standard Version (1989). A few, marked in the text, are from the New International Version (2011) (NIV), the New English Translation, v1.0 (2004) (NET) and the New Jerusalem Bible (1985) (NJB). There is one featuring the author's own amplification of the text of 1 Cor 14.1 on p15.

First Impression September 2023

ISSN 1365-490X

ISBN 978 1 78827 339 8

1

Introduction

Love is in the Air

We hear a lot about love these days. The word seems to serve many purposes from 'I love my new phone' to the fast-food chain's advertising slogan, 'I'm Lovin' It' to the easy-come, easy-go romantic love of TV shows and movies. There is no doubt that a lot of what we think about love we get from popular culture. A recently published book is entitled *Everything I Need To Know About Love I Learned From Pop Songs,* which, sadly, is probably right for a great many people.[1]

Elvis Presley sang that he can't help falling in love; Beyonce said she's crazy in love when she looks and stares so deep in your eyes; Rod Stewart sang love is the craziest thing you'll ever do. For Celine Dion, love is the one true emotion that unites us all—'people around the world, different faces, different names.' The Beatles famously sang, 'All you need is love.' And then they broke up.

Love is in the air, it's all around, says John Paul Young's hit song. In songs, TV programmes, movies, poems, books, we are swimming in love.

But the sort of love we are fed from popular culture is often a strange type of love—a kind of watered-down version, love that gratifies us, love we can fall into and out of without thinking too much. Bob Dylan hits the nail on the head in one of his gospel songs, 'You don't want a love that's pure, You want to drown love, You want a watered-down love.'[2]

There is something in us that longs for love

But despite all the watered-down ideas about love, there is something in us that longs for love, for acceptance, to be known, to be cared for. Our overall psychological well-being—the way we feel about ourselves, the quality of our relationships, and our ability to deal with difficulties—depends on a sense of being valued and loved.

Psychological studies say that love brings a sense of security and well-being, and gives us a greater sense of purpose and optimism. And neuroscientific studies indicate that when we have a sense of being loved, a powerful cocktail of chemicals is released in our brains that reduces fear and makes us feel better.

So love—not watered-down love, but real, deep, love that accepts us, that makes us secure, that delights and fulfils us—yes, and challenges us too, and makes us better people—that is something we all want, we all need.

Real Love

It is only when we turn to the Bible that we begin to understand what real love is. Love is a major theme throughout the Scriptures, but it may come as a surprise to find that it is in the letters of the apostle Paul that we find the nature of love most carefully articulated, and we discover how central it was to the establishment and growth of the church in the first century.

The love of God somehow does not feature prominently in much serious written discussion about the apostle Paul. Consult any introduction to Paul, any theology of Paul, any book specializing in some aspect of his writings and thought, or any book covering New Testament ethics, and you will find surprisingly little attention paid to this.

Justification, the nature of faith, the Law, the relationship between Jew and gentile, Paul against the background of paganism and philosophy, are all well-worn paths in Pauline studies. In places where his letters are preached there are endless sermons and discussions worrying about how precisely good works interact with faith—most springing from ideas about what Paul might be saying about salvation. Important as theological matters are in both the academy and the church, there is one theological matter the importance of which is often hugely overlooked. Paul, however, does not overlook it.

The sheer number of times in his letters where Paul refers to love—well over a hundred times, aside from related matters—ought to alert us to the fact that love was central to Paul's thinking and life. God, he says, is the God of love and peace (2 Cor 13.11). God's love has been poured into our hearts (Rom 5.5). Christ's love is beyond anything we think we know (Eph 3.19). Love was the be-all and end-all; the greatest thing in the world, for Paul, was love (1 Corinthians 13).

Love is central to Paul's thinking and life

In this Grove booklet I want to explore the theme of love in Paul's thinking, understand its importance for him and the first Jesus followers, and to see what relevance that might have for us. As we do so, I hope we will begin to agree with Patrick Mitchel's assessment of Paul as 'the apostle of love.'[3] Many of us may think such a title is more appropriate for, say, the apostle John, whose gospel and letters contain a great deal of discussion of love. Paul, however, has just as much claim to such an appellation. Love was central to his theology and practice.

The World-changing Love of God 2

The Importance of Love

Tom Wright has said that Paul's letter to the Romans 'is suffused with resurrection. Squeeze this letter at any point, and resurrection spills out.'[4] Actually, we might say the same about love. Paul starts off by addressing the Romans as 'loved by God' (something, as we will see, that must have been astonishing to Roman pagans); appeals to the assurance of God's love as the ultimate comfort to people suffering from violence, lack of food and clothing, persecution and danger (Rom 8.35); and goes on to urge loving relationships within and without the community in the latter part of the letter.

The basis for this Paul spells out in chapter 5 of the letter—the proof that God loves us is in the death of the messiah, Jesus. This is not only a fact to be reckoned with, but something to be experienced—the love of God has 'been poured into our hearts through the Holy Spirit that has been given to us' (Rom 5.5).

As Paul thought deeply about what God was doing in Christ, he saw the 'purpose and good pleasure' of God in adopting Jesus' followers as his children was because of God's love (Eph 1.4b, 5, NJB). It was the richness of God's 'great love' that resulted in God's action in Christ (Eph 2.5), something that Paul expansively refers to as 'the surpassing wealth of his grace in kindness toward us in Christ Jesus'—all the more amazing when contrasted against human weakness, sin and disobedience (Eph 2.1–7, NET).

Paul was deeply and personally aware that God loved him

For Paul, this was not just an idea or theology, it was personal. The Son of God loved *him*, Paul, he tells the Galatians in (Gal 2.20). He was deeply and personally aware that God loved him, and that God, who had not spared his own Son, and had, in his kindness, freely given him up, was 'for' him (Rom 8.32). It was a sense of this astonishing love that motivated him and spurred him on through the beatings, the floggings, the hardships of an itinerant life and the misunderstandings and rejections he often experienced—Christ's love, he told the Corinthians, 'urged him on.'

Paul's dramatic encounter with the risen, living messiah on the road to Damascus that fateful day brought his previous knowledge of the lovingkindness of

Israel's God into sharp focus. He began to understand the deep love of God for not only Israel but the world. His personal encounter with Jesus, resulting in a deep appreciation of God's love for *him*, set him on a commitment to love as way of life.

Paul's Scriptures

The idea of a loving God was one that was part of Paul's heritage as a first-century Jew. Paul knew Israel's God as a God who loved his people deeply.

People sometimes drive a wedge between the Old Testament and the New, where the God of Israel is an angry, warlike God as opposed to the loving God of Jesus Christ. To be sure, there are problems and questions to face in reading some portions of our Old Testaments. Then there is the false idea that the Old Testament is really all about demanding ritual, with a message about trying to keep the works of the law, as opposed to the New Testament's focus on grace and love.

But it would be a grave mistake to miss the theme of love running through the Old Testament. In fact, the whole Bible, both Old Testament and New, is a single story of God's relentless love for sinners.

In his faithfulness to them, God essentially and profoundly loved his people Israel through all their tortuous history, their foolishness and unfaithfulness. Again and again, God had graciously intervened on behalf of his people, and prophets like Hosea, Ezekiel and Jeremiah spoke in emotional terms about God's intense love for God's people.

In the Torah, God's love features prominently. In Exodus, in one of two foundational texts for Jews, God reveals himself as 'the LORD, a God merciful and gracious, slow to anger, and abounding in steadfast love and faithfulness' (Exod 34.6), and this after God's people had shown their own unfaithfulness in the golden calf incident. In Deuteronomy, the theme of God's constant faithful love for his people and their responsibility to reciprocate that love occurs again and again.

The other foundational text in Paul's Scriptures is Deut 6.4–5. Known as the *shema*, this is the central affirmation of Judaism and is traditionally recited twice a day. 'Hear, O Israel: The LORD our God, the LORD is one. You shall love the LORD your God with all your heart, and with all your soul, and with all your strength' (NIV).

The faith of Israel, then, was grounded, not, as is sometimes thought, primarily in rules and regulations, but in a deep sense of God's love for Israel and the obligation to reciprocate that love.

One of the main Hebrew words used for God's love is *hesed* which is usually translated 'steadfast love' or 'lovingkindness.' It refers to God's faithful, covenant love, his care for the well-being and flourishing of his people. Israel's God is said to abound in *hesed*. It is a term that appears very frequently in the Psalms, where YHWH's goodness and tenacious support is celebrated—God protects, forgives, offers comfort and care. God loves his people completely, fiercely and with utter faithfulness.

God's deep love for God's people, reflected in Deut 10.15—'The LORD set his heart in love on your ancestors alone and chose you, their descendants after them, out of all the peoples'—was balanced by the requirement in the *shema* to 'love the LORD your God with all your heart, and with all your soul, and with all your might.' Importantly, that command to love God was to be worked out in practical ways within the community, including loving the 'foreigner' (Deut 10.19).

The love of God's people for God and others is, however, clearly predicated on the prior love of God. It was God who took the initiative in choosing Israel, making her his people and delivering her from bondage. Out of such a knowledge and experience ought to spring a response of willing love from God's people.

God's covenant love for his people is also to the fore in the prophets

God's covenant love for his people is also to the fore in the prophets. In Hosea, God is portrayed as a passionate, betrayed lover who is determined to win back his unfaithful wife. Despite Israel's breaking of her covenant obligations through idolatry and toleration of deceit, murder and theft, God is still committed to her and promises: 'I will commit myself to you forever; I will commit myself to you in righteousness and justice, in steadfast love and tender compassion' (Hos 2.19, NET). God's love here is extraordinary! It is undeserved and stubborn, and risks all in pursuit of a relationship with his people. The loving nature of God, which runs like a golden thread through the Old Testament, becomes so explicit in Hosea that we gasp at its passion and relentlessness.

God's Love Extends to the Whole World

Paul's awareness of the loving nature of Israel's God became intensified, when, after personally encountering the risen Jesus on the road to Damascus, he reflected on the meaning of Jesus's death and resurrection. This, he came to see, was the surprising way in which Israel's God was fulfilling his covenant promises and expressing his faithful love.

Paul's Scriptures, which he knew well, as we have seen, had spoken to him of a God of love and faithfulness. That knowledge, however, was tied up with a sense of the peculiarity of Paul's own nation Israel and her special status as God's people. But Paul's experience of the risen Jesus and his searching of his Scriptures led him to understand the full extent of God's love, which had become manifest in the incarnation, life, death and resurrection of Christ.

What became evident to him was that God's love and his promises were not only for the benefit of Paul's own people, Israel, but were to be enjoyed and experienced by everyone. It is significant that he quotes a text from Hosea when discussing the inclusion of the Gentiles in God's plan of salvation: 'As indeed he says in Hosea, "Those who were not my people I will call 'my people,' and her who was not beloved I will call 'beloved'"' (Rom 9.24).

Hosea's words, which were intended for the wayward nation of Israel, are now harnessed by Paul to apply to the rest of the world. Paul goes on a verse later to appropriate the not-my-people becoming 'children of God' in Hos 1.10 for Gentile believers who are now welcomed warmly into God's beloved family.

Paul came to see that the incredible mercy of Hosea's God who loves and loves and loves again, is extended beyond the boundaries of the nation and includes everyone. It reaches, Paul explains, 'us, whom he also called, not from the Jews only, but also from the Gentiles' (Rom 9.23).

The love of God, Paul came to realize, encompassed all of humanity

The faithfulness, mercy and love of God, Paul came to realize, had been most powerfully revealed in Jesus, and now encompassed all of humanity. This reality gripped him and became the driving force in his life. He said Christ's love 'impelled' him so that he could no longer live for himself (2 Cor 5.14–15). The new life he experienced by being 'in' the messiah, Jesus, was because of the Son of God's love for *him* (Gal 2.19–20).

Paul and God's Love

Paul had previously been a man of considerable violence, motivated by his zeal for his ancestral traditions and clearly driven by considerable anger and hate. Fellow Jews recognized him as having 'ravaged' Jesus' followers, a term that indicates the use of considerable violence, and one that Paul himself was prepared to admit to when describing his way of life prior to meeting Jesus (Acts 9.21; Gal 1.13, 23). As a result, he considered himself in the front rank of sinners (1 Tim 1.15). Consider what he says of his previous life: 'Even though I was formerly a blasphemer, a persecutor, and a man of violence…I received mercy and the grace of our Lord overflowed for me with the faith and love that are in Christ Jesus' (1Tim 1.13–14).

The change in Paul because of meeting with the risen Jesus was dramatic. Some have referred to his Damascus road experience as a calling, God directing Paul to be God's witness to the Gentiles. While that is true and Paul does refer to this event in terms reminiscent of God's calling of Israel's prophets (Gal 1.15), it perhaps does not do justice fully to the change that took place in Paul's life.

While he never abandoned his Jewishness, and remained faithful to his Scriptures, the reorientation of his theology and understanding of the Scriptures around the messiah Jesus radically changed Paul's way of life.

Instead of anger and violence, there was now a commitment to peace; he offered blessing to his opponents instead of slander (1 Cor 4.12b); and he now had a new depth of understanding of the love command of Lev 19.18—'You shall love your neighbour as yourself.' For Paul, the whole Jewish Torah was summed up by this command and the idea of 'neighbour' extended far beyond anything he had considered to date (Gal 5.14).

Paul clearly lost none of his passionate nature but he was able to channel it into his new mission to spread the good news of Jesus the messiah. His letters portray a man zealous for his faith, willing to suffer greatly for it and quite willing to stand up for what he believed was right when the occasion demanded it. The violent, ruthless Paul, however, had been changed into a Paul motivated and shaped by his experience of the love of God. God loved him and nothing, as he wrote with considerable passion to the Romans, could ever separate him from that love.

If we ever doubted the importance of love to Paul, what he says to the Corinthians in chapter 13 of his first letter ought to be enough to convince us. Beyond those things that New Testament scholars typically highlight when talking about Paul—(justification by) faith and (eschatological) hope—Paul elevates love. These two things, along with love, are of abiding importance, but 'the greatest of these is love.'

Paul had come to experience for himself the faithful, loving God of his Scriptures

Paul had come to experience for himself the faithful, loving God of his Scriptures. The passionate, all-consuming love of God in the face of human failure and sin revealed in texts like Hosea had become a reality in the person of Christ. Jesus, he came to see, was the ultimate expression and embodiment of God's complete and utterly self-giving love.

Christ's death for us is the proof, the demonstration of God's love, Paul says in Rom 5.8. Christ died for us while we were yet sinners, God's enemies even, when we were completely alienated from God, completely unworthy of such love. Paul is so taken by this amazing turn of events that he says in Rom 8.32,

'He who did not spare his own Son, but gave him up for us all—how will he not also, along with him, graciously give us all things?' (NIV)

An experience of, and deep appreciation of, God's love shown in Christ, then, became the driving force of Paul's life and the essence of what he believed ought to characterize the little groups of Jesus' followers dotted around the Mediterranean world to which he wrote.

God's love was, as his Scriptures had taught him, to be reciprocated by a grateful people. That now, was to be the response of all peoples. Christ's love was 'for all' (2 Cor 5.14); all the Romans, both those from a pagan as well as Jewish background were 'loved by God' (Rom 1.7, NIV); and all, both Jew and Gentile, who 'loved God' (Rom 8.28) were to 'be devoted' to each other in love (Rom 12.10, NIV).

Questions to Consider

- In Romans 5 Paul points to the objective fact and proof of God's love as the death of Christ for us. He also says (v 5) that God's love has been poured into our hearts through the Holy Spirit. In what ways does the Spirit help us realize God's love in our experience?
- Paul's sense of God's love for him was the motivating factor in his life. How important is it to have such a personal sense of God's love along with a broader sense of God's love for the world?
- Does the theme of God's love in the Old Testament surprise you? What references to God's love or related themes, for example, can you find in the Psalms?

3

A World in Need of Love

The Harshness of Life in the First Century

Paul's gospel flourished in a world desperately in need of love. When Paul wrote to Jesus' followers in Rome in the middle of the first century about the incredible love of God shown in Christ, which, he said, nothing in heaven or earth and not even death could separate them from, we get a stark picture of what life was like for most people in the urban centres of the Roman Empire.

He mentions trouble, persecution, distress, famine, nakedness, danger and the sword, all hazards that face people living in poverty or near poverty then and now (Rom 8.35). In our comfortable, first-world lives we imagine that Paul here is speaking hyperbolically—how wonderful, we think, that if anyone were to face such things, they could still rely on God's love.

It is important, however, to realize that Paul's world did not have a large middle class where social mobility was commonplace, as is the case in our world. In the Greco-Roman world, perhaps only 3% of people lived comfortably—various Roman, provincial and urban elites. Another 7–15% were traders and artisans, whose lives were reasonably stable economically (but very far from the level of comfort we might imagine for business people in our world), and then the great majority of people who were either just about getting by or seriously struggling.[5]

The majority of people were just getting by or seriously struggling

The lives of the little groups of Jesus' followers dotted around the Mediterranean world were no different than the vast majority of their neighbours. Their lives were difficult and, in a crowded city like Rome, people lived in cramped apartments where there was no sanitation and the night soil was just tipped out the window. Many also lived in shanties or lean-tos, or slept rough.

Hunger was a constant problem for most people and food was often contaminated. The experience of inadequate clothing was commonplace, with repairing and patching the norm. Lack of sanitation and poor diet resulted in poor health; if you got sick, what doctors or medicine had to offer was very limited. If you became seriously ill, you would probably die.

Children and mothers died in childbirth and infant mortality was high. Disease or fire could spread rampantly through neighbourhoods. Seeing family members, friends and neighbours die was commonplace for everybody, and the vast majority of people simply lived from day to day, doing their best to survive.[6]

Life for people in the cities where Paul worked was akin to life for poor communities today in the developing world. Many people in big cities like Mumbai or Nairobi live in unsanitary conditions with rubbish in the streets, vile smells and people living in tiny rooms. So too did most of the first Christians and their neighbours.

In addition, a considerable proportion of the population was enslaved. Estimates vary but it is likely that around 30% of people in the Empire were slaves, the vast majority of whom worked in mines, on farms, in road construction and doing a host of menial tasks in households. They were considered simply as property. Abuse, including beatings and sexual assault, was common. These were people who were part of the first Christian groups, along with artisans, day labourers, craft workers, immigrant workers and homeless people.[7]

So, in chapter 8 of his letter to the Roman Christians, when Paul says, 'I consider that the sufferings of this present time are not worth comparing with the glory about to be revealed to us,' he is not talking hypothetically, or about some minor inconveniences.

Paul knew precisely the vulnerable existence of the believers in Rome and wanted them to know that the hardships they faced could not separate them from the love of Christ. The list of troubles that he lists in Rom 8.35 reflects the very real difficulties they faced:

- *Hardship*: just being able to get enough money for the basics of life, including shelter, food and clothing, could not be taken for granted.
- *Distress*: seeing your relatives, friends and children get sick and die. Twenty-five per cent of children died before their first birthday in the first century.
- *Persecution*: Jesus' followers were seen as not honouring the gods that protected their neighbourhoods. This made their neighbours suspicious of them, disinclined to do business with them, and at times actively opposing them.
- *Famine*: hunger was an ongoing problem for ordinary people in Rome, many of whom depended on a grain dole (the giving out of grain) by the authorities—though not everyone was entitled to this. Paul himself in 2 Corinthians 11 says he was 'often without food.'

- *Peril*: Rome was a city of great violence—it was a place where slaves were beaten and sexually exploited; where newborn babies were thrown away on rubbish heaps; where political and street mob violence was commonplace; and where the gladiatorial games preserved an atmosphere of violence.
- *The sword*: Rome used the sword regularly as a means of execution. Capital punishment frequently involved torture, flogging, crucifixion, dismemberment and more.

There were no social services to help people, little in the way of medical care and philanthropy or what we might think of as charity was very limited.

The Astounding Message of God's Love

Into such a world and to such people came Paul's gospel about the love of God demonstrated in Jesus Christ. This message must have been astounding, even bizarre, to people who were used to gods who were uninterested in the fate of humanity; who were capricious and at times vengeful. The gods did not love you; you just made an offering of grain or wine at a shrine and hoped that that was enough to placate them.

This was a pre-scientific world where superstition was rife, where the gods of luck or chance were worshipped and natural events blamed on the whims of the various gods.

For vulnerable individuals whose lives were seemingly of little worth and who had little control on the chaos all around, a message about an all-powerful God who had died for them, had been resurrected and who was 'rich in faithful love for them' would have sounded almost incredible (Eph 2.4, NJB).

Paul's letters are grounded in this message of God's love. He wanted the Thessalonians' hearts to be directed to the love of God (2 Thess 3.5). He prayed that the Ephesians would 'know the love of Christ that surpasses knowledge', which he said, in a telling statement about the loving nature of God, would fill them with the knowledge of God (Eph 3.19). In his benediction to the Corinthians, he prayed for God's love to be with them (2 Cor 13.13). He tells the Romans that God's love had been poured into their hearts (Rom 5.5).

All of this is predicated on the amazing fact of the death of Christ on humanity's behalf—this is the clear demonstration of God's love, says Paul, that Christ died for us while we were sinners, estranged from God, God's enemies even (Rom 5.8–10).

In Paul's world, as in ours, this was a truly amazing message: the one true God, the maker of the universe, loves and accepts each person and group without distinction or qualification, as demonstrated through Christ.

My experience of working in very disadvantaged communities in India has been that people living in poverty and desperate conditions have very low self-esteem, often not able to make eye contact with those they perceive as being of higher status. This often leads to a host of problems, both personal and social, including depression, anxiety and substance abuse.[8]

In Paul's world, which was very hierarchical and where honour and shame were dominant social values, self-esteem and a sense of self-worth for those further down the social ladder would have been very low.

Thus a message about a God who had entered into their very situation—and had himself become as a slave—because he cared for them and loved them, would have been transformational. The whole Christian message, based on the love and mercy of God, was utterly countercultural and was, for many people, wonderfully good news—particularly, as we shall see, when the message became demonstrated in practical ways within the Christian communities.

It is good news for our world as well, where even in developed societies loneliness and lack of self-esteem have become major problems and many people struggle to have a sense of being loved. We are bombarded with advertising messages every day that tell us our value depends on this or that product or experience. Social media promotes lifestyles we cannot attain to, body shapes we will never achieve and experiences we will never have.

Add that to the be more, achieve more, excessive individualism in Western society and it is no wonder that more people than ever before feel isolated, lonely and unloved.

The gospel's message of God's love for humanity and for individuals is the answer to the malaise of low self-esteem, loneliness and sense of being unloved both in Paul's world and ours. This is true especially, as we will see from Paul's letters, when God's love is made concrete through the loving lifestyles and actions of Jesus' followers.

Questions to Consider

- How do you think a message about a God who loved people would have sounded to people in the cities of Paul's world?
- How important in our world is a message about—and a demonstration of—God's love? What particular personal and societal problems does a message about God's love address?

Live in Love

4

Love Your Neighbour as Yourself

Interestingly, out of all the times Paul mentions love (over 100 times in the thirteen letters ascribed to him), he only mentions our love for God on five occasions. While he talks warmly about Christ's love for us and 'the God of love and peace,' and his whole theology is predicated upon the love of God shown in Christ, much of what Paul has to say about love is about us loving others.

Furthermore, while Paul specifically refers to love on these many occasions in his letters, that is really just the tip of the iceberg. We hear him talking again and again about forgiveness, peace, non-violence, kindness, faithfulness, forbearance and compassion. Love pervades Paul's letters. But it is all summed up by Eph 5.2: 'Live in love, as Christ loved us and gave himself up for us, a fragrant offering and sacrifice to God.' And also by 1 Cor 14.1 where Paul's Greek communicates simply, 'Pursue, seek after, strive for, love.'

Clearly Deuteronomy's instruction to love the Lord your God with all your heart, soul, and strength loomed large in his thinking but it is the instruction in Leviticus to love your neighbour as yourself, which is repeated again and again in a variety of ways, that directed the way in which Paul put love for others at the centre of Christian faith and living. The love of neighbour that sprang out of love for God in Paul's Scriptures included not only the neighbour and family, but the stranger, with a warning against injustice and taking vengeance.

Paul was also aware that Jesus had said that the supreme sign of being his follower was love, and that he had summarized the whole of the teaching of Torah in just two commandments—to love God and love your neighbour. Paul takes this up in Rom 13.9, where he says that all the commandments of the law are summed up in this word, 'Love your neighbour as yourself.' Love, he goes on to say, is the way in which the whole Jewish law becomes fulfilled.

The way of love, the pursuit of love, was, for Paul, at the heart of faith in Jesus the messiah. This was the way that faith was expressed. Commenting on Gal 5.6, Tom Wright says that Paul here is saying that the messiah's people are 'faith-through-love' people.[9] Bringing people to the 'obedience of faith' was what Paul thought was the point of his apostleship (Rom 1.5) and he spelled out the nature of such obedience later in chapter 12—showing mercy, service, hospitality, generosity, harmonious living, sympathy—in short, love for those in the community and without.

The Example of Jesus

The love of God, for Paul, had been supremely demonstrated in the self-humbling service of the messiah Jesus. That becomes crystal clear in chapter 2 of his Letter to the Philippians in the famous 'Christ hymn' in verses 6 to 11.

The passage is, of course, breathtaking in the way that Paul identifies Jesus with Israel's God. The backdrop here is a number of Old Testament texts that refer to the exaltation of the divine name above all, but especially Isaiah 45, where what is said of Israel's God—who has no peer, is the source of salvation and is the one to whom every knee will bow and every tongue swear allegiance—is now to be said of Jesus, clearly positioned within the divine identity.

That being the case, we get a remarkable insight into the nature of God. Michael Gorman makes a good case that the Greek in verse 6 has the sense of '*because* Christ was in the form of God…' as opposed to 'although…'[10] So it is precisely *because* of Christ's position as part of the Godhead that he did not think this was something to be selfishly exploited, but rather humbled himself through taking on humanity and suffering a death reserved for criminals.

This is a crucial insight into the very nature of God—utterly self-giving—in essence a nature of love. Wright says that the equality with God status that Paul ascribes to Christ is 'given its proper interpretation; not the self-aggrandizement one might have imagined, but a life of self-emptying, humble service.'[11]

Paul wants the Philippian Jesus followers to be united and of one mind

This Christ-hymn passage is the rationale Paul gives to the Philippians for his appeal for them to love one another in the earlier part of chapter 2. For the sake of love and compassion (verse 1), Paul wants the Philippian Jesus followers to be united and of one mind in allegiance to Jesus, living together selflessly. His comments in verses 3 and 4 effectively define what Paul means by love—not being motivated by selfishness or vanity, behaving in a humble manner, treating others with respect, and not focusing on one's own concerns and interests but rather those of others.

This is a far cry from our modern ideas about love, which often revolve around having loving feelings that can come and go like the ocean's tide.

Paul's kind of love is very much action-oriented and other-oriented. To make it quite plain what a life of this kind of love is like, Paul goes on to use the example of Christ. The Philippians (and we) ought to have the very same attitude as that of the Lord himself. 'Cultivate *this* way of thinking, feeling and acting,' says Paul in verse 5, and points to the example of Christ who poured himself out for others, exemplifying the ultimate self-humbling possible: Isaiah's God, who is above all, become human and suffering the most cruel and abject of deaths.[12]

This is the very essence of love, and what Paul is saying here really fills out the apostle John's stark 'God is love' (1 John 4.8). Paul sets the bar high for what the Philippians' and our love for others ought to look like—it is seeking to emulate Christ who was prepared to humble himself at the greatest cost, becoming someone without rights, privilege or advantage.

That is the sense too, of Paul's exhortation to the Galatians, where the essence of loving one another is service, and that of a most lowly kind (Gal 5.13–14). This is what Christ's love, God's love, looks like; it must be what love in the community of those who follow him looks like.

Love Among the First Jesus Followers

Again and again in his letters, Paul urged these little communities of Christians to live in ways that exhibited kindness, generosity and compassion, bearing one another's burdens and imitating the self-denying, serving love of Christ.

As we have seen, these were groups of people who lived in considerable hardship and uncertainty with few resources and where exhibiting kindness and love to people beyond your family or to social inferiors was unusual, to say the least. It must have been amazing for slaves, homeless people and hard-put manual day labourers to find themselves welcomed, afforded respect and their needs attended to, when they became part of a Jesus community. To be embraced with a holy kiss—and this in a culture where kisses were reserved only for relatives, not to be freely shared amongst members of different families, slaves, the free, men, women and children alike (Rom 16.16).

Jesus' followers found themselves in a group totally unlike anything else in the Empire. There was nothing in the worship of the pagan gods to encourage love and compassion, certainly not towards people who had nothing, and nothing to give back to you. Larry Hurtado notes that 'We simply do not know of any other Roman-era religious group in which love played this important role in discourse or behavioural teaching.'[13]

Love as Sharing in the Ancient world

In the ancient world, possibly because of the uncertainty of everyday existence, common sense dictated that a person be cautious about sharing. Several hundred years before Paul, the Greek poet Hesiod advised inviting only your friend to dine, visiting only those who would visit you and giving only to those who will give back. As Barclay says, 'There is every reason to think that the social norms outlined here were constant and pervasive in the Mediterranean world for centuries.'[14]

Gifts, favours and sharing of material goods were very much on a transactional basis, bound up with a sense of obligation or with a judgment about who might be worthy of assistance and who might be able to repay in kind. The idea of obligation and debt was strong and so sharing was usually only with those who could repay. Friendship, said Aristotle, was for those who could 'confer benefits on each other.'[15] Wealthy elites funded public buildings, temples and public feasts and events, but the purpose from their point of view was to display their generosity and gain honour in the sight of their peers and the public.

It is no surprise, then, that those on the margins—which, let us remember, was the vast majority of the population of Paul's world—were not generally included in the generosity of the well-off elite.[16] The patronage of the elite that was a feature of the Roman world generally did not extend to the poor who had nothing really to offer in return. So with nothing in the way of what we might think of as trickle-down economics or widespread support for people living precarious lives, any sort of free sharing and mutual support was not the norm—for the vast majority of people, the world in which Paul lived was uncertain, harsh and at times brutal.

Bearing One Another's Burdens

It is against this background that we must read Paul's letters and his many references to love, compassion and mutual support. Groups of people living as if the normal difference between slaves and free, men and women, and Jews and Gentiles did not matter, and finding ways to love and care for each other, would have been very countercultural, revolutionary even. Paul's vision was for a new realm that exhibited justice, peace and joy (Rom 14.17); a new citizenship, where people were not motivated by selfish ambition and treated others as more important than themselves; and where those who were currently humiliated by life could expect transformation (Phil 2.3; 3.20–21).

Despite the struggles that these groups of Jesus' followers had in forging new communities, of which Paul was well aware as he sought to address them in his letters, the love these first Christians discovered in their little communities resulted in them contributing to each other's needs, and was the thing that sustained them in the very difficult circumstances in which they lived. They 'bore one another's burdens' (Gal 6.2), helping each other in practical ways—in some cases helping each other to survive, making sure everybody had enough to eat, had clothes to wear and somewhere to shelter. They supported each other in the face of the trials that life threw at them in the cities of the Roman empire.

Food, shelter and clothing were not to be taken for granted in this world, but Paul's letters are peppered with concern that the love that Jesus' followers have experienced in Christ might be expressed in meeting the basic needs of others in the community (and beyond).

In Rom 12.13, Paul urges the Romans to 'contribute to the needs of the saints' and to 'pursue hospitality' (NET). In the same chapter, he talks about showing compassion, serving and showing mercy—all ways in which the Romans could 'be devoted to one another with mutual love' (vv 7–9, NET). In 1 Thess 5.14, Paul says simply that they ought to 'help the weak,' most likely referring to those who were economically vulnerable.

In 1 Timothy 5, Paul refers to the community's support for needy widows. In Titus 3, Jesus' followers are to devote themselves to good works in order to meet the needs around them. In Ephesians 4, we find Paul urging Jesus' followers to work so that they have enough left over to share with the needy.

In 2 Thessalonians, Paul refers to his own example of not eating anyone's food without paying for it and being prepared to work hard all hours of the day and night so as not to be a burden to people whose resources were already under strain (2 Thess 3.8). After considering the problem Paul addresses at Corinth, where some came to the communal meal with an excess of food and refused to share it with poorer community members, Campbell suggests that, 'It seems clear that Paul's communities were eating together and sharing their food together, a practice that is significant when...many people were hungry.'[17]

One other important piece of evidence that the early Christians' love was expressed in tangible and counter-cultural ways is the money collection that Paul mentions on several occasions in his letters (1 and 2 Corinthians, Galatians, Romans). This was a project that was of enormous importance to Paul, carried out, probably, in the early 50s.

Paul knew of great need amongst Jesus' followers and he wanted the Gentile Christians to help

Basically, Paul knew of great need amongst Jesus' followers in Jerusalem—possibly as a result of famine—and he wanted the Gentile Christians to help. It looks like he drove this fund-raising for several years before eventually taking the money to Jerusalem.

This collection of Paul's shows how generosity was a part of first-century faith expressed in love, especially so in that the believers whom Paul was collecting from were themselves not well off. How is it that those who are in need themselves are often much more generous than those of us blessed by so much? I remember at times being utterly humbled in visiting people in marginalized communities in India. People who had very, very little brought me food and bottled Coke that they really could not afford, just in order to be hospitable.

Enemy Love

The love that was at the centre of Paul's gospel and that was expressed in these practical ways also, importantly, included enemy love. Again, Paul takes up the teaching of Jesus who had extended the need to love others beyond neighbours to enemies.

The idea of enemy love was foreign to the rabbinic teaching that Paul inherited, and there really is no parallel in the Greek philosophical tradition. So, when Paul says in Romans 12, 'If your enemies are hungry, feed them' and 'Bless those who persecute you; bless and do not curse them,' this would have been radically different from anything the Romans had encountered.

For a vulnerable group of people on the margins and the object of considerable suspicion, with persecution an all too real possibility, this was not some hypothetical advice. The dangers facing these Christians were real. Enemies were tangible—some of those in the Roman house churches had experienced deportation from the city a few years before on account of their faith (compare Acts 18.2) —and reacting in such a way as to bless them, and help them, and love them, was something extraordinary.[18]

Given the importance of communal meals to these little groups, it may well be that Paul's advice to provide food and drink to enemies referred to inviting neighbours, and others who were hostile, to join them.

Violence permeated the world Paul lived in. Roman literature, coins and architecture were replete with violent images, attesting to the unrestrained violent nature of the Roman military. Banditry was rife, and blood feuds and personal vendettas common.[19] The appearance of a new sect that, neighbours may have thought, dishonoured the gods and thus had the potential of bringing calamity upon their neighbourhoods, doubtless earned the groups of Jesus' followers disapproval and various kinds of abuse (*eg* Phil 1.28–30). Paul himself suffered beatings and imprisonment.

Despite this, Paul, says that 'When reviled, we bless; when persecuted, we endure; when slandered, we speak kindly' (1 Cor 4.12–13). Paul trod the path of peace-making and non-violence that Jesus had trod and urged his churches again and again to be centres of peace and love that not only governed their own communities but extended to outsiders and even enemies.

Questions to Consider

- 'The way of love, the pursuit of love, was, for Paul, at the heart of faith in Jesus.' In what ways can I/my church make sure that love is central and something that others feel defines us?
- Generosity was a defining element in early Christian communities. In what ways might each of us become more generous with our time, resources and money?
- What does loving our enemies mean for each of us in our modern world? Is it possible to be faithful to the values of peace and enemy love for which Jesus and the first Christians are remembered?

5 Love Can Change the World

The Challenge of Living in Love

There is no doubt that living in a way that is characterized by love, and in particular, the same sort of self-sacrificial love shown by Jesus, is a huge challenge. For people in Paul's little churches who were just about getting by and used to guarding their meagre resources closely, sharing freely and generously might sometimes have felt like a tall order.

Paul's list of the fruit of the Spirit in his Letter to the Galatians—love, joy, peace, patience, kindness, generosity, faithfulness, all aspects of the loving lifestyle Paul urges—was, and is, utterly countercultural. His account of the meaning and content of love in chapter 13 of his Letter to the Corinthians, is incredibly challenging: 'Love is patient, love is kind, it is not envious. Love does not brag, it is not puffed up. It is not rude, it is not self-serving, it is not easily angered or resentful. It is not glad about injustice, but rejoices in the truth. It bears all things, believes all things, hopes all things, endures all things' (NET). If you have any doubts as to the high bar that Paul sets here, just try putting your own name in place of the word love in this passage, *eg*: 'Gary is patient, Gary is kind…' For the Corinthians, caught up in their petty internal divisions, competitiveness and self-centredness in worship, and also for us, caught in an increasingly individualistic way of life, Paul's description of the true nature of love can seem impossible.

Paul's description of the true nature of love can seem quite daunting

There is no doubt that this revolutionary life of love is a tall order. We have become increasingly aware of the variety of views held by different Christians on a range of theological or ethical issues through social media, and it is easy to be sucked in to the irritation and outrage that characterizes much of the interaction. At times we are so protective of our own affluent lifestyles that we become indifferent to the cries for help from people in our own locality and in the wider world. The comfort and convenience of our lives—the life of our churches even—either drown out the apostle Paul's clarion call to love in a radical way or tempt us to think that it is just too much to ask.

Paul knew that the loving lifestyle that he urged the groups of Jesus' followers to adopt was something new and revolutionary. This is why he points them and us to the example of the generosity of God and the example of Jesus. It is that example that spurs us on. But even that would not be enough to enable us to live in this revolutionary way.

But something has happened to Jesus' followers. Paul says they have become part of a 'new creation,' where the old way of life has passed away and the new has come (2 Cor 5.17). This has been made possible by the reality of the Holy Spirit, so that the life of self-sacrificing love that emulates the love of Jesus is now a possibility. Paul's list in Gal 5.22 of the love-expressing ways in which Jesus' followers are to live is termed *the fruit of the Spirit*. This is the natural outcome of people who have been regenerated and renewed by the Spirit, which has been 'poured out lavishly' upon them (Titus 3.6, NIV).

Paul talks at some length about the way in which the Spirit transforms the lives of Jesus' followers in his letter to the Romans, when he compares life in the flesh to life in the Spirit. Life in the flesh is the old, former way of life, characterized in Romans 5 by sin and death, as opposed to the new life that believers have been given in Christ.

In Romans 8, Paul says categorically that the Romans 'are not in the flesh; you are in the Spirit, if the Spirit of God lives in you' and goes on to say that the same Spirit that raised Christ from the dead indwells us.

When Paul told the Philippians that they ought to 'have the same mindset as Christ,' which he then showed was one of incredible humility and love, he very quickly assured them that working this out in practice was entirely possible because God was at work in them, not only in their action, but in their desiring. As Gordon Fee says, 'Being Christ's means...to have one's life invaded by God's Holy Spirit so that not simply new behaviour is now effected, but a new desire toward God that prompts such behaviour in the first place.'[20]

Paul's sense is that something tangible has happened to Jesus' followers

Paul's sense, then, is that something real and tangible has happened to Jesus' followers. We have been given the Spirit, the Spirit lives in us, we are led by the Spirit, God's love is poured upon us by means of the Spirit, the Spirit brings us joy and life—nothing could be clearer from the deluge of references to the Spirit that we get in Paul's letters, than that we are people indwelt by the very presence and power of God. You can understand why Paul thinks we should live as changed people, why we are no longer in slavery to sin, to a former way of life, to life in the flesh. And why he thinks it is possible for Jesus' followers to live a life of love.

Love is Joyous

You might think that living in a way that does not look to your own interests and serves others might end up being a dour struggle. Paul does not see it that way. When the indwelling Holy Spirit enables us to live in the revolutionary way of love, joy is the necessary result. Being free from self-centredness to look to the interests of others, and giving ourselves over to participate in practical ways in the generous love of God, brings a freedom and joy not possible otherwise.

Paul urged the Corinthians to 'sow generously' with respect to giving to his collection for suffering Jerusalem believers, and to contribute gladly. God, he said, loves a cheerful giver and 'is able to bless you abundantly, so that in all things at all times, having all that you need, you will abound in every good work' (2 Cor 9.6–8, NIV).

Holy Spirit-inspired joy, Paul said, is one of the natural outcomes when we let God take charge (Rom 14.17)—when his kingdom, the chief hallmark of which is love, is present. Paul talks about joy a great deal in his letters. No matter the stresses and difficulties faced by him and these groups of Jesus' followers, they had begun to participate in the very life of heaven, and the presence, life and love of Jesus amongst them brought a deep-seated and tangible sense of joy and celebration.

So they could indeed be cheerful givers, even though they had little themselves. The love and support they gave each other enabled them to survive, thrive and rejoice in circumstances we would find very challenging.

The Triumph of Love

These early Christians who read Paul's letters began to live in a new way. They started to love one another in a revolutionary way. They supported one another through the hardship, at times enabling each other to survive. They started caring for their neighbours. Before long they were getting a name for the way in which they loved each other and their communities. They were beacons of light in a dark place. They imagined their world could be different, and they began to live as if it were. Within a couple of centuries their faith had spread all over the world.

These early Christians started to love one another in a revolutionary way

Within fifty years of Paul writing his Letter to the Romans, it is reckoned that the number of Christians in the city had increased by at least four-fold—and this despite Nero's executions in the 60s. By the year 350AD, there were likely over 30 million Christians in the Roman Empire.[21] Much of this was down to the way in which these early believers modelled a transformed way of life, showing the reality of the kingdom of God to the world around.[22] Tertullian, the second-century North African Christian leader and author, said that it was his community's care of the helpless, 'our practice of loving kindness that brands us…"Only look," they say, "look how they love one another!"'[23]

Unlike any other groups in the Empire, every week, generation after generation, Christians collected money for orphans, the sick, widows and those in prisons. They stayed behind in epidemics to care for the sick when everyone else had left. Before long, well-organized networks of social security had developed, showing the world that there was a new way of being human that was based on love.

Despite the opposition at times of their neighbours and the authorities, and periodic persecution, they proved that the power of God's love is greater than violence or any earthly power. God's love enabled them to change the world.

The sort of love so casually talked about, sung about and portrayed in popular entertainment—what Bob Dylan called 'watered-down' love as we noted earlier—is a far cry from this sort of world-transforming love. For Paul, this love was centre and foremost in his understanding of what God had done in Christ and was seeking to do in the world through Jesus' followers. Love is the most powerful force in the universe. It is the 'greatest thing' and it 'never ends.'

Can we, then, imagine a world transformed by the love of God? A world experiencing the peace of God? Can we imagine our own lives and church communities breaking out of the old mould of the world's self-centredness, greed and inequality? Of course, we know that the wholesale transformation of the world awaits that final day of God's renewing of the cosmos. But can we imagine some of that into the present and see it become a reality, by lives characterized by generous, joyful, self-denying and serving love?

> Live in love, just as Christ also loved us.
>
> Eph 5.2

Questions to Consider

- Read 1 Corinthians 13 and substitute your own name for love. What can you do to address those aspects of love that seem to be a challenge?
- Does the clarity of Paul's emphasis on a radical life of love make us uncomfortable? What aspects of modern life make it difficult for us to follow a life of love more fully?
- Is it possible to live such a life? What might enable us to do so?

Bibliography

If you would like to follow up this theme of love in Paul's letters further, I would particularly recommend the following, in addition to the works cited in the notes:

G W Burnett, *Paul Distilled* (Eugene, OR: Wipf and Stock, 2021)

D A Campbell, *Pauline Dogmatics: The Triumph of God's Love* (Grand Rapids, MI: Eerdmans, 2020)—especially chapters 11–15

P Mitchel, *The Message of Love* (London: IVP, 2019)—especially chapters 8, 9 and 14–17

P Mitchel, 'Love,' in S McKnight, L Cohick and N Gupta (eds), *Dictionary of Paul and His Letters (2nd edition): A Compendium of Contemporary Biblical Scholarship* (Westmont, IL: IVP, 2023) pp 663–669

Notes

1 L Roberts, *Everything I Need To Know About Love I Learned From Pop Songs* (Createspace, 2016).

2 Bob Dylan, 'Watered-Down Love,' from his 1981 album *Shot of Love.*

3 P Mitchel, *The Message of Love* (London: IVP, 2019) pp 12, 119.

4 N T Wright, *The Resurrection of the Son of God* (Minneapolis, MN: Fortress Press, 2003) p 241.

5 For sustained discussion of this, see S J Friesen, 'Poverty in Pauline Studies: Beyond the So-called New Consensus,' *JSNT* 26 (2004): pp 323–361; P Oakes, *Reading Romans in Pompeii: Paul's Letter at Ground Level* (SPCK: London, 2009); B Longenecker, *Remember the Poor: Paul, Poverty and the Greco-Roman World* (Grand Rapids, MI: Eerdmans, 2010).

6 For a discussion of the conditions in which people in the Empire of the first century lived, along with supporting sources, see J J Meggitt, *Paul, Poverty and Survival* (Edinburgh: T and T Clark, 1998).

7 P Oakes, *Reading Romans in Pompeii, op cit.*

8 The effect of poverty on self-esteem, confidence and mental health is well attested: *eg* D Z Reyles, 'The ability to go about without shame,' *OPHI Working Paper NO 03* (May 2007): 'Shame and humiliation are central to the understanding of poverty'; B Fell and M Hewstone, 'Psychological Perspectives on Poverty,' (Joseph Rowntree Foundation, June 2015): 'Poverty increases the risk of mental illnesses, including schizophrenia, depression, anxiety and substance addiction.'

9 N T Wright, *Galatians* (Grand Rapids, MI: Eerdmans, 2021) p 439.

10 M J Gorman, *Becoming the Gospel* (Grand Rapids, MI: Eerdmans, 2015) p 107f.

11 N T Wright, *Paul and the Faithfulness of God* (London: SPCK, 2013) p 686.

12 M J Gorman, *Participating in Christ* (Grand Rapids, MI: Baker, 2019) p 87f.

13 L Hurtado, *Destroyer of the Gods: Early Christian Distinctiveness in the Roman World* (Waco, TX: Baylor, 2016) p 65.

14 J M G Barclay, *Paul and the Gift* (Grand Rapids, MI: Eerdmans, 2015) p 25.

15 Aristotle, *Ethica Nicomachea* 1157b7–8.

16 Longenecker, *Remember the Poor, op cit*, carefully sifts the evidence for charity in the first century and, while presenting a complex and nuanced picture, nevertheless says that there were but 'low level forms of care for the poor in the ancient world' and 'the elite were generally not involved in efforts to offset poverty,' pp 66, 107.

17 D A Campbell, *Pauline Dogmatics: The Triumph of God's Love* (Grand Rapids, MI: Eerdmans, 2020) p 283.

18 Claudius' expulsion of Jews from Rome in AD 39 is reported by the Roman historian Suetonius as 'on account of Chrestus,' widely taken to refer to Christ.

19 J Gabrielson, *Paul's Non-Violent Gospel* (Eugene, OR: Pickwick, 2013) p 7f.

20 G D Fee, *Paul's Letter to the Philippians* (Grand Rapids, MI: Eerdmans, 1995) p 238.

21 R Stark, *The Rise of Christianity* (New York: HarperOne, 1997) p 10.

22 H Chadwick, *The Early Church* (Harmondsworth: Penguin, 1967) p 56: 'the practical application of charity was probably the most single potent cause of Christian success' in the first few centuries.

23 Tertullian, *Apologeticus*, ch 39.